Paying EVIL TITHES

DR. D. K. OLUKOYA

Warfare Prayer Series 15

Paying The Evil Tithes

DR. D. K. OLUKOYA

D. K. OLUKOYA

PAYING THE EVIL TITHES
© 2005 DR. D. K. OLUKOYA
ISBN 978-38205-1-6
1st Printing - July 2005 AD

Published by:
The Battle Cry Christian Ministries
322, Herbert Macaulay Street, Sabo, Yaba, P. O. Box 12272, Ikeja, Lagos.

Phone: 0803-304-4239, 01-8044415

All Scripture quotations are from the King James Version of the Bible

Cover illustration: Sister Shade Olukoya

All rights reserved.

We prohibit reproduction in whole or part without written permission.

TABLE OF CONTENTS

PAYING THE EVIL TITHES 4

FEEDERS OF STRONGMAN 13

DEALING WITH THE RAGGING SPIRITS . 27

PARALYSING WICKED REVIVAL 41

D. K. OLUKOYA

CHAPTER ONE

PAYING THE EVIL TITHES

Pray these prayer points before you continue.

1. Every destiny padlock, die, in the name of Jesus.

2. Every power of ancestral witchcraft; what are you waiting for, die, in the name of Jesus.

3. Every witchcraft surgery, backfire, in the name of Jesus.

1 want you to read an uncommon passage of the

PAYING THE EVIL TITHES

scriptures. It is found in the book of Hebrews 7:9-10.

Hebrews 7:9-10: And as I may so say, Levi also, who receiveth tithes, payed tithes in Abraham. For he was yet in the loins of his father, when Melchisedec met him.

It was Abraham who gave birth to Isaac. And Isaac gave birth to Jacob. Jacob was the one who gave birth to Levi, one of the twelve sons of Jacob.

Levi was one of the patriarchs. The Bible has a very interesting information for us, that Levi paid tithes when he was in the loins of Abraham, when Abraham paid tithes to Melchisedec. The tithes Abraham paid to Melchisedec was also on behalf of Levi. That is the spiritual reason of exempting the Levites from the payment of tithes. Just as this incidence was positively applicable, so also it could be negatively applicable.

THE DEVIL'S LEGAL CLAIM

Many of our forefathers had paid tithes to the devil, while our grandfathers were yet unborn. The full implications of this now stare us in the face. Levi was in his father's loins when the deed of payment of tithes was carried out. This deed paid off for the Levites, because it was a positive act of faith for Abraham to pay tithes to

Melchisedec, king of Salem.

What happens when negative tithes had been paid by an offspring through his progenitors? What happens to the children and grandchildren of those, who paid tithes to the devil? The simple answer to this question is that the enemy has legal claims on such people, and will trouble them sore.

THE FATHER PLANTED AND THE SON REAPED

Our hope of deliverance from such generic bondage is found in Isaiah 49:24-25:

Shall the prey be taken from the mighty, or the lawful captive delivered? But thus saith the Lord, Even the captives of the mighty shall be taken away, and the prey of the terrible shall be delivered: for I will contend with him that contendeth with thee, and I will save thy children.

Some people have described man as the architect of his own fate. Some have described man as the master of his own destiny. While most of these assertions cannot be outrightly discarded, it would be educative to learn that man is most of the time bombarded with many forces which he does not understand.

PAYING THE EVIL TITHES

Many of these forces cannot be naturally controlled by his efforts. The Bible makes it clear, that man will reap what he sows, also makes it explicit that man can reap what he did not sow directly. The fathers could sow hatred and the children reap wickedness. A dead man might have planted evil seed which the children would reap later. A man may sin, and the children may suffer the full penalty of the sin committed.

At this point, I would like you to make the following prophetic statement: "I refuse to reap any evil harvest, in the name of Jesus."

This explains, why we should be careful, and watch our actions. These can affect innocent souls. The things you do, either good or bad, have a long time implications.

You must tailor your life according to God's pattern, because what we do today, affect generations after us.

Many are presently suffering from intense frustrations. They cannot understand what is going on. Perhaps their ancestors have frustrated the good effort of others. And now, their children are caught up with nemesis. They have paid evil tithes and the children are reaping the results.

There is another uncommon verse in Genesis 15:16

But in the fourth generation they shall come hither again: for the iniquity of the Amorites is not yet full.

Do you notice that there are many unstable homes now? It may be that your mother or grandmother was forced on your father or grand father. The woman was never happy in that house. In such an instance, tithes were paid, and someone would have to reap the effects of evil tithes.

Have you noticed incessant failure in business? Is there not a reason why an uneducated person sells a product with a good profit margin, but inspite of the education of another fails at business? This might be due to the fact that your father or grand father, was making money fraudulently. And, the cup of his iniquity is now full. This is a serious matter.

In 1995, a man came to a church, where I was invited for deliverance. The man wept bitterly after the message on rapture. He did not explain to anybody why he was crying. The next day he came to the church with a bag. Inside the bag were hundreds of local rings, together with charcoal and other things. At every market day, the man would go to the market and start to market his products with a bell and megaphone saying, "If anybody

PAYING THE EVIL TITHES

puts poison in your food and you put on this ring, you will know because a lizard will jump out of your food". Every market day, the man sold fake rings to people.

The man confessed that the rings were fake, because they have no power to deliver anyone from food poison. The man then used the money of reward of iniquity to send his children to school. The two children failed woefully at school. The children were nowhere to be found academically, because their father used fraudulent money to train them.

I want you to pray this prayer point before you continue with the reading. "Thou power of God, go to my foundation now, in the name of Jesus"

Are you enriched with dirty money? Such as the money received from pool and gambling business, smuggling and prostitution? It may be that your father was a commercial prophet, and has sponsored your education from the proceeds of such business. It might be that your father projected himself to people as a seer, thereby collecting money and materials from people. These are all forms of evil tithes, that could be detrimental to your growth and progress in life.

You may have great health problems, because you

sprang up from a family of idolatry. It might be that your early childhood, was spent in the house of witches, who were feeding you with human flesh and blood. Those things, which you have consumed, might now be consuming you internally.

Do you notice continuous nightmares? This might be the result of parental witchcraft. Are you so prone to experiencing tragedies? It may be because your parents used protective charms on you, when you were young. The demons from such deeds might be making you to pay evil tithes now.

HOW SHALL WE ESCAPE?

The first basic and initial step towards deliverance, is to surrender your life completely to Jesus. You must repent from any personal sins, which you are committing now, so that you will no longer be suffering from tithes, paid in an evil manner.

The villagers in a certain place gathered together, to appeal to an idol to give them rain for their crops. The idol agreed to send them rain on the agreement that they stop eating traditional African okro soup. They all agreed and entered into a covenant with the god, that

PAYING THE EVIL TITHES

from that time, nobody from that village would eat okro, and that anybody who would go contrary to the vow, would develop epilepsy. If somebody from such village who now stays in the city starts to eat okro, he will develop epilepsy, unless the power of Christ delivers him. The members of such a community will pay evil tithes, even if they study overseas.

Therefore, repent from your personal sins. Then, go ahead to confess the sins of your ancestors. Acknowledge that there was a problem, and pray to disconnect yourself from the evil ladder.

John the Baptist was filled with the Holy Ghost from his mother's womb according to Luke 1:15.

For he shall be great in the sight of the Lord, and shall drink neither wine nor strong drink; and he shall be filled with the Holy Ghost, even from his mother's womb.

The negative part of this could also be possible, a child could be sold out to the devil from the womb. You must set yourself free from evil tithes today.

PRAYER POINTS

1. Every platform of failure constructed by my father,

I pull you down, in the name of Jesus.

2. Oh thou that troubleth my Israel, my God shall trouble you today, in the name of Jesus. Thou earth, vomit my virtues, in the name of Jesus.

3. Every ancestral power of witchcraft, release my destiny, in the name of Jesus.

4. Every ancestral cage, break, in the name of Jesus.

CHAPTER TWO

FEEDERS OF STRONGMAN

It is a sin to be kind to satan. It is criminal to be merciful to the enemy of your soul. Therefore, I want you to pray with this mind set, before you commence your reading.

1. By the powers that destroyed Goliath, Oh God, arise, and fight for me, in the name of Jesus.

2. Every Goliath witchcraft, every pharaoh witchcraft, what are you waiting for, die, in the name of Jesus.

3. Every arrow shot against my breakthroughs, backfire, in the name of Jesus.

There are two passages that are very crucial to this topic. The first is located in Matthew's gospel;

Matthew 12:29: Or else how can one enter into a strong man's house, and spoil his goods, except he first bind the strong man? and then he will spoil his house.

There is a power, known as the strongman. The strongman has a house, loaded with goods. The goods are stolen, because they do not belong to him. If not, there would be no attempt, to take them back from him.

To recover the stolen goods from the strongman therefore, he must be bound, before his house is spoilt. There is always a supervising power or strongman over every stubborn situation. This is one of the few lessons, which can be picked on the surface from Matthew 12:29.

Let us go through an Old Testament passage, relevant to this study in Zechariah 11:9.

Then said I, I will not feed you: that that dieth, let it die; and that that is to be cut off, let it be cut off; and let the rest eat every one the flesh of another.

PAYING THE EVIL TITHES

This quotation reveals exactly how the Lord wants us to deal with our strongman. The strongman must not be fed. Our enemies need not be fed. It is unfortunate that many of us feed our enemies, thereby giving them more strength and fortitude to fight us.

If your enemies must die, let it be so. Never feed your enemies. If they are to be cut off all the same, let it be, but to feed the enemies, God forbid! It would gladden my heart if the rest enemies, who did not die of hunger, perished by killing themselves, eating their own flesh, and drinking their own blood.

This message is a revelation of victory and it is quite revelational. It will deliver into your hands cheap victory over all the troublers of your Israel. It will make you triumph over your enemies come with ease.

WHEN A PROBLEM DEFIES SOLUTION

A man was a member of a particular church. He had a serious problem, that seemed to defy any solution, including prayer. The man went from pillar to post, in search of solution, but to no avail.

He tried several fetish priests, including those, who press the sand, as a means of divination, yet, there was no solution in view. He had wasted all he had, on searching for all possible human solutions to the problem. He had forgotten God, the Controller of the whole universe. Instead of his situation to improve, it became worse.

One day, his younger sister came around and promised to take him to another fetish priest, who could easily help him. They went to the fetish priest. The fetish priest brought out his oracle, in order to divine. The fetish priest then said; "Excuse me sir, go back to your church, there is sufficient power there to set you free". The man said; "But I know there was a church, before I came to you. Why couldn't you just help me out?" The fetish priest said; "I must tell you the plain truth, that your case is beyond my capacity. Only the church people can handle it."

To the amazement of the man, the fetish priest quoted a Scripture he has never heard before. The fetish priest said; "Have you not read it in the book of Genesis that when thou art strong, thou shall remove the yoke off thy neck?"

The fetish priest then concluded; "Go for the power, then you will be able to remove the yoke from your neck". The kind of problem this man faced was

PAYING THE EVIL TITHES

stubborn. It will require nothing, but God, to deliver such a person. When a problem defies solution, it means there is an evil personality called the strongman, supervising such a problem.

There are technical prayers to be prayed in such instances, to dislodge the enemy in charge of the problem. Sometimes such strongman drives people to despair and discouragement, so that they will think that God is no longer answering prayers, and that he has forgotten them.

I got interested in the plight of a particular blind man sometimes ago. He was a nice man. So, I took it upon myself to be praying for him. The first day I prayed for him, he could see, and even was able to point to the buttons of my clothes. With this development, I felt I should continue praying for him, until there is perfection of the miracle in his life.

One day I went there and I told the man to bring out all the charms and fetish power he was using. He brought them out, and I burnt them on his behalf. So, our prayer continued on a very good note.

I was surprised one day, when I got there to pray, only to discover that the case had gone worse. He could not see again at all! I cried unto God, "Why has this happened again?" Then God spoke to me, and said; "If you want to know the source of the problem, pay a surprise visit to the man by 12:00a.m."

So, instead of meeting the man at the normal time scheduled for prayer, I decided to go by midnight. When I got there, I saw the man with a strange woman on his bed, yet, I was praying with the man for a miracle. Little did I realize that he had a strongman that was standing against him.

In the kingdom of darkness, there are many evil departments, such as yoke-replacement-department, the department of resurrection of afflictions, the regrouping department and the recruitment department. Therefore, a believer, who is praying, against replacement, regrouping and recruitment, is praying an effective prayer.

Before you continue, I want you to pray this three-in-one prayer. "There is no reinforcement, there is no replacement, and there is no regrouping for my strongman, in the name of Jesus."

It is a prayer like this, that can give a total breakthrough to an individual. When the strongman is totally dealt with, total and resounding breakthroughs would be the result.

It is, therefore, a major disaster for a person to start feeding the strongman, instead of killing him.

THE FEEDERS OF STRONGMAN

This is the catalogue of men and women, who feed their strongman.

☞ The Ignorant

Many do not know what to do, and how to do it. Many are completely unaware of how far the strongman has gone. There are men and women, whom the enemy has blinded. Satan has closed their ears to the fact that there is an entity called the strongman. Some people will tell you that the devil does not exist. They are ignorant people. They deny the existence of witches and wizards. Those, who believe in the existence of these beings, will go ahead to tell you that you do not need to pray against them, since Jesus paid it all, and ended it when He said that "it is finished" on Calvary.

Such ignorant people are giving food to their strongmen.

☞ The Unbelievers

The Bible says, "that some heard the word of God, but are destroyed, because the word they heard did not mix with faith in them." That is why the word did not prosper them. The act of unbelief will feed the strongman. If you still believe that there is nothing drastic that could happen to you positively, inspite of reading such a powerful book as this one, then, you are feeding the strongman. If you are praying without specific expectation, then you are feeding your strongman.

Do you expect great things to come across your way, or are you expecting to hit your jackpot as in gambling or lottery? As you are feeding the devil, the strongman is happy anytime you doubt God. If you want to walk with God, it must be done by faith and not by sight. If you depend on your five senses, you will not be able to defeat the strongman.

Faith knows no impossibility. It does not believe in the doctor's report. Faith only believes the word of God. If doctors are saying something, and the Bible is saying something entirely different, faith will only cling to the word of the Lord. Faith recognizes facts, but chooses to believe the truth of the word of God.

PAYING THE EVIL TITHES

You ought to renounce the spirit of unbelief and proclaim your faith. The more you speak words of faith, the more your spirit is lifted.

☞ The Unrepentant

There is another group of people who feed their strongman. They live and pride in unconfessed sin. They refuse to bring their sins to the limelight, so that God can deal with them.

Let us read Proverbs 28:13.

He that covereth his sins shall not prosper: but whoso confesseth and forsaketh them shall have mercy.

Some people think that God is unaware of their sins, if they can hide them, and refuse to confess them. It is quite impossible to hide anything from God. Our innermost secrets are not hidden from Him. See what the Psalmist said:

Psalm 139:1-5: O Lord, thou hast searched me, and known me. Thou knowest my downsitting and mine uprising, thou understandest my thought afar off. Thou compassest my path and my lying down, and art acquainted with all my ways. For there is not a word in my tongue, but, lo, O Lord, thou knowest it altogether. Thou hast beset me behind and before, and laid thine hand upon me.

That secret sin that you refuse to confess and forsake, will serve as food to energise, the strongman against you.

These sins could be anger, lust, gluttony or fornication. As soon as they are not confessed and forsaken, you are feeding your enemies.

In one of my recent ministerial travels to England I saw two different cartoons in the British newspapers, trying to convey a message. The first cartoon portrayed a man, who was rushing to the church, but his suit was withheld by the devil, so as to hinder him from getting to the house of God.

The second cartoon has to do with a man, who was drunk. There were bottles of beer, under the table of the man. A demon, who was fast asleep, was under his table, too. It was fast asleep without realizing what was going on. This means that the demon had accomplished his work and now he was resting. This depicts the picture of the lives of so many people.

What God expects from you is to confess your sins and forsake them, so as to obtain mercy. Once this is done, the strongman would be starved to death.

Failure to forgive is another serious sin that could feed the strongman. Every act of un-forgiveness and resentment is a feeder to the strongman.

That is why the Lord commands that whenever we are to pray, we should forgive.

Mark 11:25: And when ye stand praying, forgive, if ye have ought against any: that your Father also which is in heaven may forgive you your trespasses.

Decide and make up your mind to forgive.

☞ Occult Involvement

God abhors occultism and idolatry. He does not want His people to get involved. He warns sternly against these practices. Look at God's instruction against these practices below;

Exodus 23:25: And ye shall serve the Lord your God, and he shall bless thy bread, and thy water; and I will take sickness away from the midst of thee.

Several people put on things that are bewitched from the occult kingdom. Men and women who put on these things identify themselves with the demonic world unconsciously. Most of the earrings, necklaces, and midget sculptures, which people put on today, have demonic influences backing them up. It is ironic that many of us use our money to purchase bondages for ourselves.

The Egyptian culture has so many sculptures, which are put on in form of ornaments and jewelleries. All these things have their satanic names. Once you get yourself involved in the transaction and usage of these ornaments, you get entangled and you start to strengthen your strongman against yourself.

I had a cause to pray for a family that was bewitched. After prayer, one of the daughters in the family confessed to her involvement in witchcraft. The first thing she spoke that amazed her mother was about the necklace. She said; "Mummy, bring out the necklace you bought from Thailand." The mother went inside and brought out the necklace. The girl said; "This necklace is not the one you bought from Thailand, I have exchanged the one from Thailand for another one in the demonic world. The one you are using now is demonic and is from the water. This is the cause of your hypertensive mood."

This illustrates the fact that what most people put on ordinarily are not just ordinary. They are backed up by demonic forces. You cannot come up to say you want to bind the strongman, when his properties are found in you.

PAYING THE EVIL TITHES

Our environment is so polluted and spiritually contaminated, that we need both inner and outward purity, in order to survive the attacks of the enemy.

The source of troubles in your life and family, might be because of what you put on.

If you have got involved in cultism, such as the pirates confraternity in the university, and you still have their properties with you, you have got to do away with them.

If prior to your conversion, you were involved in fetish power of any kind, you have to renounce them, and burn their objects. That was exactly what happened to the believers in Christ in the Acts of the Apostles.

Acts 19:18-19: And many that believed came, and confessed, and shewed their deeds. Many of them also which used curious arts brought their books together, and burned them before all men: and they counted the price of them, and found it fifty thousand pieces of silver.

All inherited jewelleries and artifacts from our dead parents and relatives should be relinquished and destroyed for the sake of total deliverance from the strongman that is parading the garden of your life.

☞ **Covenant and strange gods**

Entering into a covenant with strange gods will strengthen the strongman against your life.

Exodus 23:32: Thou shalt make no covenant with them, nor with their gods.

From today, stop feeding your strongman, but rather fight him hard and get yourself free from his domain. Do not treat the strongman with levity, instead with force. Deal with the strongman with the weapons of prayer and fasting and you will see him fizzle out of your life

PRAYER POINTS

1. Ancestral strongman, release my destiny, in the name of Jesus.

2. Ancestral strongman, die, in the name Jesus.

3. Stubborn strongman, attached to my family, what are you waiting for, die, in the name of Jesus.

CHAPTER THREE

DEALING WITH THE RAGGING SPIRITS

Pray these prayer points loud and clear.

1. Mountain of worry, I bury you, in the name of Jesus.
2. Mountain of doubt, I bury you now, in the name of Jesus.
3. Mountain of frustration, I bury you now, in the name of Jesus.

4. Arrows of wickedness fired into my life, die, in the name of Jesus.

5. I arise above negative circumstances, in the name of Jesus.

6. Every arrow of shame, working against my life, die, in the name of Jesus.

7. Wherever the enemy has knocked me down, I arise by the power of God, in the name of Jesus.

8. Every Goliath of my father's house, die, in the name of Jesus.

9. Let every power divining against me, receive madness, in the name of Jesus.

10. Let any power delegated against my progress die, in the name of Jesus.

11. The sun shall not smite me by day nor the moon by night, in the name of Jesus.

12. Let every power covering my glory die, in the name of Jesus.

I want you to carefully reed this passage:

Mark 9:17-27: And one of the multitude answered and said,

PAYING THE EVIL TITHES

Master, I have brought unto thee my son, which hath a dumb spirit; And wheresoever he taketh him, he teareth him: and he foameth, and gnasheth with his teeth, and pineth away: and I spake to thy disciples that they should cast him out; and they could not. He answereth him, and saith, O faithless generation, how long shall I be with you? how long shall I suffer you? bring him unto me. And they brought him unto him: and when he saw him, straightway the spirit tare him; and he fell on the ground, and wallowed foaming. And he asked his father, How long is it ago since this came unto him? And he said, Of a child. And ofttimes it hath cast him into the fire, and into the waters, to destroy him: but if thou canst do any thing, have compassion on us, and help us. Jesus said unto him, If thou canst believe, all things are possible to him that believeth. And straightway the father of the child cried out, and said with tears, Lord, I believe; help thou mine unbelief. When Jesus saw that the people came running together, he rebuked the foul spirit, saying unto him, Thou dumb and deaf spirit, I charge thee, come out of him, and enter no more into him. And the spirit cried, and rent him sore, and came out of him: and he was as one dead; insomuch that many said, He is dead. But Jesus took him by the hand, and lifted him up; and he arose.

If the enemy is raging against you, it means, there is something in your life that is worth contesting for. You may not know, or discover the treasures that are in you, but dark powers can see it.

It is not a sign of a bad omen, when there are several attacks targeted against you. It is a sign that there is a glorious deposit in you, that the enemy is envious about. Confess this: "My virtue shall not be stolen, in the name of Jesus."

Why was the boy referred to in the text as being dumb? Why did he suffer from birth? It was not because of his sins, or those of his parents. It was because there are deposits in him that the enemy is contesting for. There are things God has loaded this boy with, which got the enemy angry. Of course, the boy was innocent from birth.

By the time this boy was taken to Jesus, the demon became more angry saying; "Why was I brought face to face with this man?" What was the result of this rage?

Mark 9:20: And they brought him unto him: and when he saw him, straightway the spirit tare him; and he fell on the ground, and wallowed foaming.

When the boy was brought to Jesus, the sprit dealt with him the more. It tore him. It's anger became outrageous.

THE POWER OF FAITH

The father of the child was worried. He cried for help from the Helper of the helpless. He sought for help from the right source. Jesus gave him a specific, but general solution to the problem at hand. He said: "If thou canst believe, all things are possible to him that believeth." "All things." Every spiritual package, that is ready for delivery, is on the basis of faith. "If thou canst believe". Faith is the key. Faith is "Now." For the Bible says in the book of Hebrews 11:1: "Now faith is the substance of things hoped for, the evidence of things not seen."

Your miracles, deliverance, healings and breakthroughs, shall be delivered to you on the platter of faith.

The father of the boy keyed in into faith. He put his faith into action. He manifested total surrender to the faith in Christ Jesus, and straightway he said; "Lord I believe; help thou my unbelief."

COME OUT AND ENTER NO MORE

The Lord of lords then swung into action and rebuked the foul spirit saying; "Thou dumb and deaf spirit, I charge thee, come out of him, and enter no more into him." Make this confession loud and clear: "Come out and enter no more."

The following prayer points will grant you victory over raging spirits.

1. Every power of infirmity, come out and enter no more, in the name of Jesus.
2. Every power of death, come out and enter no more, in the name of Jesus.
3. Every power of failure, come out and enter no more, in the name of Jesus.
4. Every power of backwardness, come out and enter no more, in the name of Jesus.
5. Every power of hardship, come out and enter no more, in the name of Jesus.
6. Every power of poverty, come out and enter no more, in the name of Jesus.
7. Every arrow of witchcraft, come out and enter no more, in the name of Jesus.
8. Every mark of hatred, come out and enter no more, in the name of Jesus.
9. Every spirit of lack of promotion, come out and enter no more, in the name of Jesus.
10. Every arrow of insanity, come out and enter no

PAYING THE EVIL TITHES

more, in the name of Jesus.

11. Every arrow of curses, come out and enter no more, in the name of Jesus.

THE HEIGHT OF THE RAGE

What was the result of the statement, "Come out and enter no more into him?" How did the prayer command affect the evil spirit?

Mark 9:26: And the spirit cried, and rent him sore, and came out of him: and he was as one dead; insomuch that many said, He is dead.

The demon thought; "If I am not allowed to stay in the body of the boy to continue my work, then let me kill him."

The demon tried to execute his plan, but failed. The demon tore the boy and struck him so much that the people thought the boy was dead. But, what did Jesus do?

Mark 9:27: But Jesus took him by the hand, and lifted him up; and he arose.

The aggressive command of Jesus made that demon more angry.

Why do these demons get angry? It is because they are about to loose their accommodation. They will not be able to stay in that body again. They would have to search for another body to possess. This means that if the enemy is not smiling at you, then your prayers are getting results.

WHO ARE THE RAGING SPIRITS?

They are the spirits that show resistance to your command.

They operate with terrible anger.

They threaten and boast.

They speak strange words to your spiritual life.

They are the ones who say; "Do not bother to pray, it will not be answered."

They are violent spirits, who are responsible for dream attacks.

They are sponsored by satanic agents to carry out specific assignment.

They are spirits sponsored by incantations, curses and covenants. When you issue command unto them and say, "Leave this place." They will respond by saying that curses and covenants have given them access to operate.

Raging spirits are spiritual armed robbers.

They have no regard for geographical locations.

They can get to anywhere their targeted victims go on the surface of the earth.

They have the sole mission of killing and destruction. They are envious spirits.

They roam around the garden of life, with the aim of destroying.

They can also be referred to as dog's spirit that bites. They bark and bite.

They wage a lot of battles against their victims, when they are at the verge of deliverance and breakthroughs.

They swallow victory and destiny.

They are organized attackers.

They are spirits on assignment set to hinder at all costs.

They are spiritual dogs, sniffing out their preys.

These stubborn pursuing spirits are the raging spirits.

It will be outright foolishness to think that since you are from a Christian home, or that you never offended anybody, and you are very nice to everybody, therefore, the enemy will not attack you. This is a spiritual fallacy.

It may amaze you that you cannot find more than 15% of the people, who are free in any particular congregation or assembly.

The bitter truth is that millions of normal, respectful people are under attack every day. Battles are going on day and night. You must deal with these raging spirits.

IDENTIFYING RAGING SPIRITS

Raging spirits, who are troubling the existence and essence of man, are called problem-expanders. They move in to blow man's problems out of proportion.

Raise your voice to pray: Every power raging against my destiny, your time is up, die, in the name of Jesus.

Another raging spirit is star-hijackers. They will steal people's star, and give it to someone else.

PAYING THE EVIL TITHES

A friend of mine lived in a house for many years. In that house there was nobody whoever bought a new car. There was no naming ceremony. There was no celebration. Those who brought vehicles into the house could not afford tyres. Most of the tenants were always fighting their wives. It was terrible until the day God spoke to my friend, and said; "If you want to know where your problem lies, there is a star hijacker in the house. Go and pour your anointing oil inside the well in the compound." He did.

As the anointing oil hit the water inside the well, a live tortoise came out and floated. The brother brought it out and on the body of the tortoise were fetish things. The brother plucked off these fetish things.

Surprisingly, on the body of the tortoise was scribbled the names of all the tenants, apart from the landlord's name. The landlord was instrumental to hijacking the stars of the tenants. That was a raging power at work.

Another raging power are the coffin spirits. They pursue people in order to kill them. Their victims see death in their dreams.

Another raging power is satanic arrow. They are targeted at people.

Another raging spirit is the spirit wives and husbands, who have destroyed their victims.

Territorial powers are also part of the raging spirits. They set limits for people saying, "Nobody in this territory must make progress." If anybody tries to make progress, they will fight him hard in order to protect the embargo they have laid.

Another class of raging spirits are seducing spirits. Many of them are around in the cities and all over the places. They are seducing people both day and night. You need to obtain your deliverance.

Another raging spirits are witchcraft recruitment spirits. The way and manner these spirits recruit youths are alarming.

I once read a story from a Nigerian newspaper. The incident took place in the northern Nigeria.

There was a particular school, where ninety percent of the students were possessed. Terrible things began to happen in the school. The teachers decided to take the students to a woman in that state, who happened to be a deliverance minister. She is a lady evangelist. Just as the woman started to rain Holy Ghost fire on these children, terrible witchcraft confessions were made by

PAYING THE EVIL TITHES

the kids. It was horrible. What I found very interesting in the newspaper's report was the testimony of the daughter of the chief witch doctor in the community. Her father was the chief native doctor. The daughter was possessed.

As prayer was going on, the father came and said; "Please, help me to deliver her." The girl confessed that she had finished her father. It is amazing that a witch doctor could allow his daughter to be subjected to deliverance ministration.

Raging spirits are recruiting people for their wicked works. That is why care must be taken on what, how and where you eat.

Another ragging spirits are spiritual gunmen. They are busy shooting people in the dream. These spirits must be dealt with today.

Psalm 2:1-9: Why do the heathen rage, and the people imagine a vain thing? The kings of the earth set themselves, and the rulers take counsel together, against the Lord, and against his anointed, saying, Let us break their bands asunder, and cast away their cords from us. He that sitteth in the heavens shall laugh: the Lord shall have them in derision. Then shall he speak unto them in his wrath, and vex them in his sore displeasure. Yet have I set my king upon my holy hill of Zion.

I will declare the decree: the Lord hath said unto me, Thou art my Son; this day have I begotten thee. Ask of me, and I shall give thee the heathen for thine inheritance, and the uttermost parts of the earth for thy possession. Thou shalt break them with a rod of iron; thou shalt dash them in pieces like a potter's vessel.

PRAYER POINTS

1. Rod of God, arise in your anger and fight for me now, in the name of Jesus.

2. Every power raging against my progress, die, in the name of Jesus.

3. Strangers of darkness, release my life and die, in the name of Jesus.

CHAPTER FOUR

PARALYSING WICKED REVIVAL

Let us read psalm 27:2-3

Psalm 27:2-3: When the wicked, even mine enemies and my foes, came upon me to eat up my flesh, they stumbled and fell. Though an host should encamp against me, my heart shall not fear: though war should rise against me, in this will I be confident.

A sister was preparing to travel. She did not know that as she was planning to travel, so also some powers were planning to terminate her life. A decision was made in the spiritual realm to confuse the driver of the vehicle, which she would board. Their plan was to make the driver spiritually deaf and dumb, by ignoring the warnings of the passengers. The enemy targeted only one person, yet, he was ready to waste about sixty people's lives, who boarded the luxury bus. This is the wickedness of the evil worker.

Thank God for the life of this sister, who did not go out that day until she prayed. One of the confessions she made was the above passage.

What happened immediately they got into the vehicle? The driver started to over speed. The passengers pleaded with the driver, "Mr. Man, take it easy, our journey is just to a nearby town, hence there is no need for you to over speed."

The driver parked the vehicle and said: "Look, if any of you had done wickedly, and thereby afraid of dying, let such a person drop here". And he started to over speed as usual. A man inside the luxury bus came again from the rear, and told the driver: "Driver, we are not contending with you for over speeding. but, the point is that whenever you get to a gallop, please, try to reduce your speed, so as to carefully meander away from the potholes."

Again, the driver parked and ordered the man to get down. By this time the sister sensed an impending danger coming, she started to communicate with heaven in an unknown language. The sister was totally unaware of the fact that a development was in the offing, as a result of the enemy's determination to get at her.

It is not until you offend the wicked or evil doers before they start to afflict you. The wicked just takes interest in wicked acts. It has become part of the nature of the devil, to perpetrate these wicked works.

A lady made some strange confessions one day in the church. She locked up her mother in sickness for about thirteen months. The doctors were totally confused concerning what was going wrong with the mother, because they were unable to discover the source of her sickness. "Why did you inflict your mother with such sickness? The girl was asked; her answer was shocking: "My mother misbehaved."

She also said: "Mother would cook liver, kidney and the flesh of animal in the soup. Instead of giving me the best part of the meat, she would always give me cow skin. That was what made me angry."

When people get into trouble, you will probably overhear them saying: "I do not know whom I have offended, I do not even know my offense." It is not until you offend, before the enemy tries to attack you. You are the target of the enemy's attack, not because you have done anything wrong, but because the enemy is addicted to evil.

The word of God has bad news for the wicked. Let us consider these scriptures to see what God says about the wicked:

Job 8:22: They that hate thee shall be clothed with shame; and the dwelling place of the wicked shall come to nought.

Job 11:20: But the eyes of the wicked shall fail, and they shall not escape, and their hope shall be as the giving up of the ghost.

Job 18:5: Yea, the light of the wicked shall be put out, and the spark of his fire shall not shine.

Psalm 7:11: God judgeth the righteous, and God is angry with the wicked every day.

Psalm 146:9: The Lord preserveth the strangers; he relieveth the fatherless and widow: but the way of the wicked he turneth upside down.

Isaiah 3:11: Woe unto the wicked! it shall be ill with him: for the reward of his hands shall be given him.

PAYING THE EVIL TITHES

Isaiah 48:22: There is no peace, saith the Lord, unto the wicked.

Isaiah 57:20: But the wicked are like the troubled sea, when it cannot rest, whose waters cast up mire and dirt.

Jeremiah 30:23: Behold, the whirlwind of the Lord goeth forth with fury, a continuing whirlwind: it shall fall with pain upon the head of the wicked.

The above are God's testimonies for the wicked. No human pen wrote down any of these scriptures. They are God's final verdicts on the lives of the wicked.

We are in the last days. God has declared that in these last days, several evil things will take place. The Bible predicts that in the last days there would be fear and distress. There shall be lawlessness. There will be corruption all over. Men shall be lovers of money. Lovers of themselves. Wicked acts shall increase. There is going to be an unprecedented satanic revival, in the realm of the spirit. The devil will carry out his final attacks on human beings.

Such attacks are prevalent in the society now. Many of the things read in the newspapers could get anyone scared and fearful. The Bible says, when all these things are happening, they are just like a tip of an iceberg. "These are the beginning of sorrows."

Global peace has remained elusive. It will remain so, until Jesus Christ comes back to reign. The only peace available is for those, who belong to Jesus.

It is, therefore, saddening, for a believer to behave as a dog chasing its tail. He will continue chasing, without catching up with it. The devil is unleashing its final bullet on the human race. The devil knows that his time is quite short. Hence, he fights relentlessly to achieve his utmost destructive intention. Believers need to be more serious and focussed, in order to frustrate satan's evil intentions. Many mighty believers are falling. There are many people, who are already struck by the darts and arrows of the enemy. The Bible tells us, "Woe to the inhabitants of the earth and of the sea! For the devil is come down unto you, having great wrath, because he knoweth that he hath but a short time."

To reinforce the assertions made so far concerning the last days, read;

1 Tim. 4:1-3: Now the Spirit speaketh expressly, that in the latter times some shall depart from the faith, giving heed to seducing spirits, and doctrines of devils; Speaking lies in hypocrisy; having their conscience seared with a hot iron; Forbidding to marry, and commanding to abstain from meats, which God hath created to be received with thanksgiving of them which believe and know the truth.

PAYING THE EVIL TITHES

The devil's attack is desperately wicked. You ought to save yourself from this wicked generation. Whatever you do must be done militantly. Bible reading and praying must be done in a military way, because we are on warfare ground.

In a very good church, it is expected that half of its congregation should have received the baptism of the Holy Ghost, with the evidence of speaking in tongues. In a church that is considered to be weak, about fifteen percent might have received the baptism of the Holy Spirit. The more there are believers in a congregation with fire, the hotter the church. And, the less there are believers in a church with baptism of the Holy Ghost, the weaker the church.

2 Thes. 2:7-10: For the mystery of iniquity doth already work: only he who now letteth will let, until he be taken out of the way. And then shall that Wicked be revealed, whom the Lord shall consume with the spirit of his mouth, and shall destroy with the brightness of his coming: Even him, whose coming is after the working of Satan with all power and signs and lying wonders, And with all deceivableness of unrighteousness in them that perish; because they received not the love of the truth, that they might be saved.

Evil is getting repressed, because there are believers, who are still calling upon the name of Jesus, day and night. There is an anticipated time, when every sincere believer shall be evacuated from the earth. They shall be removed and the whole world shall be plunged in darkness; for no one shall call upon the name of the Lord again to repress evil. Then, there will be the unleashing of the forces of darkness, and unprecedented satanic power. This is what is called the great tribulation. It is better to read and have ahead knowledge of the great tribulation, than to experience it. Inspite of the potency of the name of Jesus, the devil still finds one way, or the other, to release its attack on human race. The situation will be worse, after the rapture of the saints might have taken place. It is the Church that is halting the mystery of iniquity, which is at work already.

Let us examine a similar reference in 2 Timothy 3:13

But evil men and seducers shall wax worse and worse, deceiving, and being deceived.

It is very glaring that men are becoming more wicked. People collect sand from under people's feet. They also pack faeces, in order to use it against their victims.

There was a sister, who was harassed. She was under the surveillance of her husband. Her husband confined her to the bedroom. Anytime she came home, she had to go straight to the bedroom, and remained there. She was

PAYING THE EVIL TITHES

not happy with the development. Hence, she came to me for prayer.

I gave her prayer points that were related to her problem. She noticed that a wall gecko was biting her leg, when she was praying using the prayer points. The wall gecko was holding tight to the leg, and would not let her go. The sister slapped it down and it started to run. The sister released the fire of God on the wall gecko, and it could not run fast again. That was how the sister killed the wall gecko. Is that not an act of wickedness? Who will ever suspect, that a wall gecko could be an instrument of wickedness?

There are people, who send serpents and other reptiles to other people. We have witnessed the confessions of people, who drained other people's blood. Some people's blood are already stored in satanic blood banks, unknown to them. People steal pictures, under-wears belonging to someone else and would keep them for years for evil purposes.

A man had three wives. The husband suspected one of them as the killer of a child, whom he loved dearly. So, it was decided to consult the family idol in order to identify the killer. They approached the family idol, which revealed: "This matter is beyond my capacity, try a greater god." They went to consult a bigger idol in the forest. It was the first wife, who killed the child. But the big idol was confused and picked the last wife who was innocent. She was not the killer. This is wickedness upon wickedness.

Have you discovered that people with insanity are on the increase in the society? This is not ordinary. It is a satanic manifestation. Many believers are getting confused. Many of them have discovered, for the first time in their lives, that the people, who were instrumental to their bondage had died. They are then confused as regards how to secure relevant information, that can assist them in deliverance.

Many are bewildered and are wondering, when things would be alright in their lives. "Why is it that nothing was working, and any thing which works, does so for a short time? What have I done against these wicked forces?" The only answer to these questions, is that satanic entities are holding revival. It is left for you to counter their revival with your own revival. God expects better things from us, as Christians than we are doing now.

There are so many believers, who are retrogressing gradually. Some are on fire today, the next day they have become ice-block. God is still as old fashioned as ever. His standard remains unchanged. What He said before, He is still ringing it out now. God has not, and cannot be, modernized. His requirements are the same.

There are so many churches in Nigeria now, yet there is so much corruption. There are several unimaginable occurrences, taking place, inspite of so many bishops, reverends and prophets in the land. God is interested in real Christians, who carry the fire of God. We need the fire of the Holy Ghost to quench satanic fires, that are on a rampage lately. God is looking for a deep Christian and never a shallow one. He is loathsome with cosmetic Christianity, without root.

If you are trusting God for spiritual breakthroughs, you are expected to put in a concerted effort, and follow certain steps. Those steps will open you up to the pipeline of the Holy Spirit, so that God could use you, for His revival to spring up from your life.

The devil loves it, that the names of Christians be written on the list of casualties of spiritual warfare. Let the satanic kingdom feel the impact of divine fire. The scripture says: "Ye shall know the truth and the truth shall make you free." If you are ignorant of the truth, then, you will remain in bondage. Here comes an opportunity for you, to throw stones on your spiritual Goliath, and paralyze him.

For divine revival to take place in your life, you need fire that is potent enough to paralyze satanic revival. Certain things must give way. Brokenness and submissiveness must be in place. Jesus says, that if anyone wants to be His disciples, he must deny himself. That is the first condition. Second, he must carry his cross daily, and then follow Him.

There are certain things that seem legitimate, that must be denied for the sake of the gospel. These things must be avoided. Paul said, "Why do you not suffer yourself to be defrauded?" Taking up your cross means aligning your personal opinion with the demands of God, as revealed in His word.

Pray these prayer points now.

1. Let every satanic fire prepared against my life, be quenched, in the name of Jesus.

2. I paralyze every satanic embarrassment, in the name of Jesus.

3. Let every satanic embarrassment, be paralysed, in the name of Jesus.

PAYING THE EVIL TITHES

Once God has uttered a word, then there is no power capable to cancel the word of His mouth. If God has not made a pronouncement, it is understandable, but immediately He pronounces anything, then it is binding and efficacious. If household wickedness had put unholy fingers in every department of your life, the fingers must be cut off.

The principle of God does not change. What is that principle? The principle is, "There is no peace saith my God to the wicked". Perhaps, evil pursuers were pursuing you from birth, which does not change God's testimony, that says, "There is no peace, saith my God, to the wicked." Has the world made you a shadow of whom you should become? It might be traced to certain wicked acts.

A sister was not making much profit from her business. This led her to false prophets, who gave her sponge. She did not realize that the sponge given to her was collected from a woman, who had a problem. So, her virtue was transferred, through a sponge to somebody else.

There is no peace to the wicked, not withstanding the location of the wicked. The spiritual robbers might have gone away with the blessing allotted for you. Are you facing pressures from every quarter, as a result of which your names have been circulated among wicked diviners? Yet, God has not changed His stand about the position of the wicked. There is definitely no peace to the wicked.

Are you threatened with anticipated destruction? Did unbelievers ridicule you? Are satanic agents sharing your destiny in the witchcraft market? There is good news for you. There is no peace for the wicked. Your oppressors and tormentors will crumble at your feet, in Jesus' name. Amen.

Woe betides any vessel, that is designed to harass and torment a child of God. God is good. There is no creature, that can challenge God's authority and succeed. God is good, and any force opposing God cannot prosper. Those, who are rising up against the children of God, are doomed. They must crash and crumble.

Consider what David, the psalmist, said about the wicked: "Why do heathen rage, and the people imagine a vain thing?" And he went further; "Why the kings of the earth set themselves, and the rulers take counsel together, against the LORD, and against His anointed", adding, "Thou shall break them in pieces, thou shall

PAYING THE EVIL TITHES

dash them with a rod of iron."

At this juncture, I want you to verbalize this prayer point before you continue enjoying your reading. "Let every assignment and design of the oppressors, be dashed to pieces in the name of Jesus."

Read the book of Exodus 11, from verses 3 to 8:

Exodus 11:3-8: And the Lord gave the people favour in the sight of the Egyptians. Moreover the man Moses was very great in the land of Egypt, in the sight of Pharaoh's servants, and in the sight of the people. And Moses said, Thus saith the Lord, About midnight will I go out into the midst of Egypt: And all the firstborn in the land of Egypt shall die, from the firstborn of Pharaoh that sitteth upon his throne, even unto the firstborn of the maidservant that is behind the mill; and all the firstborn of beasts. And there shall be a great cry throughout all the land of Egypt, such as there was none like it, nor shall be like it any more. But against any of the children of Israel shall not a dog move his tongue, against man or beast: that ye may know how that the Lord doth put a difference between the Egyptians and Israel. And all these thy servants shall come down unto me, and bow down themselves unto me, saying, Get thee out, and all the people that follow thee: and after that I will go out. And he went out from Pharaoh in a great anger.

This is a wonderful prediction from Moses, that the Egyptians, the enemies of God's children, were still coming to bow to Moses, and would, eventually, beg the people of the Lord to go. Did it not happen? Yes, of course, it did much happen.

Psalm 136:12: With a strong hand, and with a stretched out arm: for his mercy endureth for ever.

Pharaoh was a stubborn enemy, who required a strong hand, and a stretched out arm, before he could be silenced.

I bid you to pause again, and punctuate your reading with this explosive prayer point. "Let God arise with a stretched out hand, against my Pharaoh, in the name of Jesus."

Sometimes ago, a Pentecostal church was about to be sited in a particular town. The church leadership went to the king, to ask him for a location to erect a church building. The king being a mean person, did not want to give them a piece of land for that purpose in a good location. He thought, within himself, on how to drive away these church people, without necessarily incurring their anger. There was a particular forest, where dead pregnant women were dumped in a form of ritual, to appease the idols of the land.

In that bad bush, lived one light complexioned man,

PAYING THE EVIL TITHES

who fed on raw dog meat. Sometimes, when the man came out of the forest, fresh blood would be noticeable all over his face. There was no man, who could tell how this man got to the forest. The king wanted to play a trick on the Christians, and so, he allotted that particular forest, where the light complexioned man resided, to the Christians to erect their church building.

The Christians received the land, with much thanks from the king. The next day, the Christian entered into the bush, and prayed a fire brand prayer, after which they started clearing the bush. The first set of trees they cut, after falling down, rose up again. The Christians prayed fire brand prayers again, quoting several scriptures. It was then those who cut the trees were not able to stand upright again. They cleared the forest and started fellowship.

The yellow man came out confused and started to ask irrelevant questions such as "What is the name of your father?" He eventually threatened them to leave, or else he would foment troubles with them.

He asked them, "Who gave you this land?" They said, "The king." "That king must be mad," responded the man. The yellow man got to the king, "Are you the one, who allotted the place I dwell to some people?" "No."

The king denied. "No, I did not. You can go ahead and do anything within your power to deal with anyone who trespasses the land," the king advised the demonic man.

The man went back. He went and met the Christians, and started to make incantations. The Christians allowed him to end his chants. After making several incantations and pronouncements, the Christians said; "By God's authority we gather all the incantations and pronouncements which you have made, we baptise them with the fire of the Holy Ghost, and we transfer them to you, in the name of Jesus." The man fled and by the time he came back the next day, he had sustained a great wound on his legs. That was how the man disappeared from that town. That marked the beginning of the Holy Ghost revival in that community.

When evil men carry out their manifestations and calculations, in order to carry out their evil plans, they will fall. Why? They have forgotten that here is an invisible eye, beholding their plans and strategies, ever before they execute them. God has power to make the enemy miscalculate, and thereby enter into trouble.

The psalmist said, "I have pursued my enemy and have overtaken them, and neither do I turned back until they are consumed." It is time for you to pursue and

PAYING THE EVIL TITHES

overtake. It is time for you to say, "No", to the oppressor.

You cannot be a winner, when you spend all your time, complaining and confessing evil things. It is not possible to experience victory, as long as you are walking in the territory of satan. Losing hope cannot make you a winner. You are only a winner if you stand firm and fight. It is possible, that over the years you were cheated, but now, it is left to you, to come face to face, with the reality of God's word, which says, "When my enemies came upon me, to eat my flesh, they stumbled and they fell". You have the opportunity to command the opposing forces, to oppose themselves in your life.

A brother was appointed to die. A sister, who was helping him to fetch water in the house went to the fetish doctor to plan his death. The fetish doctor said, "People like us do not make mistakes, we bite and kill without a remnant, but in order to make sure that this plan does not backfire, let me ask a question from you." He said, "Have you ever quarrelled with the man, whom you want to kill?" The woman said, it is practically impossible to offend the man, adding that she had done all her best to quarrel with him, but all to no avail. The fetish doctor then advised her not to do anything against him.

This is a lesson for people of God not to allow for the slightest provocation. Because the devil is looking for opportunities to attack and he is ready to seize any opportunity to strike.

There was a man, who gave a testimony, that related to his past life in sin, and in the kingdom of darkness. He was given a particular juju that when he slapped somebody with it, the person would fall down, vomit and die. Before he settled the bill of the fetish doctor, he wanted to go and exercise the potency of the juju first. He took the evil ring and went to the marketplace, looking for someone who would look for his trouble.

To his amazement, he could not find someone with who he could make trouble in the marketplace. He purposely stamped somebody at the feet, hoping that the person would pick up a quarrel against him. Instead of picking a quarrel with the man, the person started pleading, though he was innocent. When he could not find someone, on whom he could test the juju he then tested it on a dog, by slapping the dog. The dog laid flat on the floor, and died on the spot. That is wickedness. You could see how far the people of the world could go to bring their evil plans to fulfilment.

A believer, who is looking for promotion, does not

PAYING THE EVIL TITHES

need to go and bow down before an agent of the devil. A Christian sister needs not turn herself to the second wife of her boss, because she needed promotion. There is no cause to pull anyone down, in order to be promoted. It is sheer waste of time and energy, to change your name and bear another person's name, for the sake of promotion. The point is this; promotion comes from God. One thing that is very sure is that there is no one, that can kill you, if you are a child of God except God has finished with you.

PRAYER POINTS

1. I paralyze the host of wickedness encamped against me, in the name of Jesus.

2. Let my good things the enemy has taken away from my life, be returned immediately, in Jesus' name.

3. Let every wicked spirit surrounding me fall into their own wickedness, in the name of Jesus.

4. Let the spirit of wickedness attached to the place of my birth, be disgraced, in the name of Jesus.

Other Publications by Dr. D. K. Olukoya

1. Be Prepared
2. Breakthrough Prayers For Business Professionals
3. Brokenness
4. Born Great, But Tied Down
5. Can God Trust You?
6. Criminals In The House of God
7. Contending For The Kingdom
8. Dealing With Local Satanic Technology
9. Dealing With Witchcraft Barbers
10. Dealing With Hidden Curses
11. Dealing With The Evil Powers of Your Father's House
12. Dealing With Unprofitable Roots
13. Deliverance: God's Medicine Bottle
14. Deliverance By Fire
15. Deliverance From Spirit Husband And Spirit Wife
16. Deliverance of The Conscience
17. Deliverance of The Head
18. Destiny Clinic
19. Drawers of Power From The Heavenlies
20. Dominion Prosperity
21. Evil Appetite
22. Facing Both Ways
23. Family Deliverance
24. Fasting And Prayer

Other Publications by Dr. D. K. Olukoya

25. Failure In The School Of Prayer
26. Freedom From The Grip of Witchcraft
27. For We Wrestle . . .
28. Holy Cry
29. Holy Fever
30. How To Obtain Personal Deliverance (Second Edition)
31. How To Pray When Surrounded By The Enemies
32. Idols Of The Heart
33. Is This What They Died For?
34. Limiting God
35. Meat For Champions
36. Overpowering Witchcraft
37. Paying The Evil Tithes
38. Personal Spiritual Check-up
39. Power Against Coffin Spirits
40. Power Against Destiny Quenchers
41. Power Against Dream Criminals
42. Power Against Local Wickedness
43. Power Against Marine Spirits
44. Power Against Spiritual Terrorists
45. Power For Explosive Success
46. Power Must Change Hands
47. Pray Your Way To Breakthroughs (Third Edition)
48. Prayer Rain

Other Publications by Dr. D. K. Olukoya

49. Prayer Strategies For Spinsters And Bachelors
50. Prayers To Move From Minimum To Maximum
51. Prayer Warfare Against 70 Mad Spirits
52. Prayers To Destroy Diseases And Infirmities
53. Praying Against The Spirit of The Valley
54. Praying To Dismantle Witchcraft
55. Release From Destructive Covenants
56. Revoking Evil Decrees
57. Satanic Diversion Of The Black Race
58. Silencing The Birds of Darkness
59. Smite The Enemy And He Will Flee
60. Spiritual Warfare And The Home
61. Strategic Praying
62. Strategy Of Warfare Praying
63. Students In The School Of Fear
64. The Dangerous Highway
65. The Enemy Has Done This
66. The Evil Cry of Your Family Idol
67. The Fire Of Revival
68. The Great Deliverance
69. The Internal Stumbling Block
70. The Lord Is A Man Of War
71. The Mystery of Seduction
72. The Prayer Eagle

Other Publications by Dr. D. K. Olukoya

73. The Problems of Incomplete Deliverance
74. The Pursuit of Success
75. The Seasons of Life
76. The Star In Your Sky
77. The Secrets of Greatness
78. The Serpentine Enemies
79. The Slow Learners
80. The Snake in The Power House
81. The Spirit Of The Crab
82. The Tongue Trap
83. The Way of Divine Encounter
84. The Wealth Transfer Agenda
85. The Vagabond Spirit
86. Unprofitable Foundations
87. Victory Over Satanic Dreams (Second Edition)
88. Violent Prayers Against Stubborn Situations
89. War At The Edge of Breakthroughs
90. When God Is Silent
91. Wealth Must Change Hands
92. When You Are Knocked Down
93. Woman! Thou Art Loosed.
94. Your Battle and Your Strategy
95. Your Foundation and Destiny
96. Your Mouth and Your Deliverance

Other Publications by Dr. D. K. Olukoya

97. Adura Agbayori (Yoruba Version of the Second Edition of Pray Your Way to Breakthroughs)
98. Awon Adura Ti Nsi Oke Nidi (Yoruba Prayer Book)
99. Pluie de Prières
100. Esprit Vagabondage
101. En Finir avec les Forces Maléfiques de la maison de Ton Père
102. Que l'envoûtement perisse
103. Frappez l'adversaire et il fuira
104. Comment recevoir la délivrance du Mari et de la Femme de Nuit
105. Comment se delvrer soi-même
106. Pouvoir Contre les Terroristes Spirituels
107. Prières de Percées pour les hommes d'affaires
108. Prier Jusqu'à Remporter la Victoire
109. Prières Violentes pour humilier les problèmes opiniâtres
110. Le Combat Spirituel et le Foyer
111. Bilan Spirituel Personnel
112. Victoire sur les Rêves Sataniques
113. Prayers That Bring Miracles
114. Let God Answer By Fire
115. Prayers To Mount With Wings As Eagles
116. Prayers That Bring Explosive Increase
117. Prayers For Open Heavens
118. Prayers To Make You Fulfill Your Divine Destiny

119. Prayers That Make God To Answer and Fight By Fire
120. Prayers That Bring Unchallengeable Victory and Breakthrough Rainfall Bombardments

ALL OBTAINABLE AT:

- 322, Herbert Marcaulay Street, Sabo, Yaba, P. O. Box 12272, Ikeja, Lagos.
- MFM International Bookshop, 13, Olasimbo Street, Onike, Yaba, Lagos.
- IPFY Music Konnections Limited, 48, Opebi Road, Salvation Bus Stop (234-1-4719471, 234-8033056093)
- All MFM Church branches nationwide and Christian bookstores.

Paying Evil Tithes

The mystery of foundational or ancestral bondage is an area of spiritual warfare which multitudes need to address more than ever before. The fact that a lot of deeply rooted problems are inherited from ancestral lines has remained a mystery. The devil has used this as an instrument to subject billions of people all over the world to all kinds of demonic attacks.

The author has therefore given practical guidelines concerning what it takes to avoid paying evil tithes. Each chapter pulsates with the anointing which breaks such demonic yokes. This book is a must read for those who are bent on saying goodbye to the payment of any form of evil tithes.

About the Author

Dr. D. K. Olukoya is the General Overseer of the Mountain of Fire and Miracles Ministries and The Battle Cry Christian Ministries.

The Mountain of Fire and Miracles Ministries' Headquarters is the largest single Christian congregation in Africa with attendance of over 120,000 in single meetings.

MFM is a full gospel ministry devoted to the revival of Apostolic signs, Holy Ghost Fireworks, miracles and the unlimited demonstration of the power of God to deliver to the uttermost. Absolute holiness within and without as spiritual insecticide and pre-requisite for heaven is openly taught. MFM is a do-it-yourself Gospel Ministry, where your hands are trained to wage war and your fingers to do battle.

Dr. Olukoya holds a first class honours degree in Micro-biology from the University of Lagos and a PhD in Molecular Genetics from the University of Reading, United Kingdom. As a researcher, he has over seventy scientific publications to his credit.

Anointed by God, Dr. Olukoya is a prophet, evangelist, teacher and preacher of the Word. His life and that of his wife, Shade and their son Elijah Toluwani are living proofs that all power belongs to God.

978-38205-1-6

www.ingramcontent.com/pod-product-compliance
Lightning Source LLC
LaVergne TN
LVHW051200080426
835508LV00021B/2721